Jimmy Carter

Jimmy Carter

Deborah Kent

AMERICA'S
39TH
PRESIDENT

Children's Press®
A Division of Scholastic Inc.
New York / Toronto / London / Auckland / Sydney
Mexico City / New Delhi / Hong Kong
Danbury, Connecticut

Library of Congress Cataloging-in-Publication Data

Kent, Deborah.
    Jimmy Carter / Deborah Kent.
       p. cm. — (Encyclopedia of presidents)
Includes bibliographical references and index.
 ISBN 0-516-22975-3
   1. Carter, Jimmy, 1924– —Juvenile literature. 2. Presidents—United
States—Biography—Juvenile literature. I. Title. II. Series.
E873.K46 2005
973.926'092—dc22   2004017772

CHILDREN'S PRESS and associated logos are trademarks and or registered
trademarks of Scholastic Library Publishing. SCHOLASTIC and associated
logos are trademarks and or registered trademarks of Scholastic Inc.
1 2 3 4 5 6 7 8 9 10 R 14 13 12 11 10 09 08 07 06 05

Contents

One   7
The Morning Bell

Two   23
To See the World

Three   37
Peanuts and Politics

Four   47
From Atlanta to Washington

Five   63
The Greatest Challenge of All

Six   81
Citizen Jimmy Carter

Presidential Fast Facts   96
First Lady Fast Facts   97
Timeline   98
Glossary   100
Further Reading   101
Places to Visit   102
Online Sites of Interest   103
Table of Presidents   104
Index   108

Chapter 1

Close to the Soil

Every morning an hour before sunup, one of the workers on the Carter farm rang a large brass bell. The clang of the bell woke the Carter family and the rest of the farmhands, calling everyone to morning chores. As a small boy, Jimmy Carter rose every morning when the bell announced the beginning of a new day.

Jimmy Carter's parents, Earl and Lillian Gordy Carter, owned 350 acres (140 hectares) of farmland near the village of Archery and about 3 miles (5 kilometers) from the town of Plains in southwestern Georgia. Atlanta, the state's capital and largest city is 160 miles (258 km) to the north, and the Alabama border is about 50 miles (80 km) to the west. The Carters raised several crops—cotton, pecans, and especially peanuts. Like all farm children, Jimmy was expected to help with chores. He chopped firewood for the kitchen stove and drew

Jimmy Carter's boyhood home on the peanut farm near Archery, Georgia.

water from the well in the backyard. He helped his father in the fields, plowing, planting, hoeing, and harvesting.

"My most persistent impression as a farm boy was of the earth," Jimmy Carter wrote years later. "There was a closeness, almost an immersion, in the sand, loam, and red clay that seemed natural, and constant. The soil caressed my bare feet, and the dust was always boiling up from the dirt road that passed fifty feet [15 meters] from our front door." Though the farmhouse had no electricity or running water, Jimmy was not aware of hardships. His childhood was a happy one, filled with hard work and rough play, and nurtured by a loving family.

Earl's Boy

James Earl Carter Jr. was born in Plains, Georgia, on October 1, 1924. He was the oldest of four children. In years to come, he would gain two younger sisters, Gloria and Ruth. Their brother Billy Carter, born in 1937, was the baby of the family.

Jimmy's mother, known to everyone in the community as Miss Lillian, was one of the rare women of her day who combined managing a farm family with a career. In addition to caring for her children and helping on the farm, she worked as a registered nurse at a nearby hospital. When Jimmy came home from school, his mother was not usually there, but she left notes on a table in the front room for him and his sisters. The notes gave them instructions about chores and homework. The Carter children later teased Miss Lillian by claiming that the little black table in the front room was their real mother when they were growing up.

Jimmy was especially close to his father, and hungered for his approval. One of his earliest memories involved a day when he was four years old. His father took him, his mother, and his little sister Gloria to see their newly purchased farmhouse. The door was locked, and Jimmy's father had forgotten the key. He managed to pry up a window, then asked Jimmy to slide through the narrow opening. Jimmy opened the door from the inside and let the others in. "The approval of my father for my first useful act has always been one of my most vivid memories," he later wrote.

Earl Carter taught his son to fish, hunt, and play baseball. Most of all, Jimmy's father taught him the importance of hard work. From an early age Jimmy knew that his contributions were needed and valued. Earl Carter didn't heap praises on his son, but he gave him the nickname "Hot Shot." When his father called him Hot Shot, Jimmy felt that he had done well.

One day when Jimmy was twelve, a long splinter pierced his wrist while he was trying to catch a chicken for the family's dinner. For days he could not

Miss Lillian Carter with her daughter Gloria and son Jimmy, who was then about seven years old.

raise his hand or bend his fingers without intense pain. It was midsummer and every hand was needed to pick cotton, but Jimmy's injury kept him from working in the fields. Finally his father remarked in disgust, "The rest of us will be working while Jimmy lies here in the house and reads a book." After his father left, Jimmy gritted his teeth and, fighting through the pain, forced out the splinter. Then he jumped on his bicycle and pedaled out to the field. He was thrilled when his father said, "It's good to have you back with us, Hot."

Working the Land

After the Civil War, thousands of poor white farmers and African Americans recently freed from slavery had no land. Those who had their own mules and farm equipment became tenant farmers, renting land from landowners. When the crops were sold, the tenant farmer paid his rent for the land.

Poorer farmers, who had only their labor to offer, became sharecroppers. A landowner would rent the sharecropper mules, equipment, and a shack to live in. He might also lend the sharecropper money for food and other necessities. At the harvest, the landowner took half or more of the proceeds from selling the crop as rent for the land. In addition, he collected further payments for equipment, housing, and loans. Often the sharecropper had no money left after his debts were paid. He was forced to remain a sharecropper the next year, often falling more and more deeply into debt.

☆ ★ ☆

Though Jimmy worked hard, he had plenty of time to play, too. Many of his friends were the children of African American sharecroppers who worked on the Carter farm. Together, they ran barefoot through the woods and fields, hunting rabbits, climbing trees, and splashing in creeks and muddy ditches. Jimmy ate and often slept at his friends' houses, and became deeply connected to their families.

Black and White

When Jimmy Carter's African American friends came to his house, they entered by the back door and ate in the kitchen. *Segregation*, or separation of white and black people, was a familiar part of life. All African Americans knew that they must not enter a white family's house by the front door or expect to eat with white people in the dining room. Public places were segregated, too. There were separate restrooms and drinking fountains labeled "White" and "Colored." At movie theaters, blacks sat in a balcony reserved for their use only. On public buses, black passengers were required to sit in a special section at the back. White and black children went to different schools. Black children were not allowed to swim in "Whites Only" swimming pools on hot summer days even if there was no swimming pool for them. By law or custom, most African Americans could not register to vote, run for public office, or serve on juries.

As he was growing up, Jimmy Carter took segregation for granted. "I don't remember ever questioning the *mandatory* [legally required] racial separation, which we accepted like breathing or waking up in Archery every morning," he recalled. During his lifetime the laws and customs of segregation would change in ways he could scarcely imagine.

Pulpits and Politics

Nearly everyone in and around Plains, Georgia, was either a Baptist or a Methodist. The Carters were Baptists, and the Baptist Church was one of the most powerful influences in Jimmy's life. The church was a major social center in the community. It sponsored family picnics and parties for teenagers. It organized fund-raisers to support overseas missions. If a church member was sick, the congregation brought food and helped with household and farm chores. When someone died, the church supported the bereaved family with condolences and prayers.

The biggest event in the church calendar was the annual *revival*, held just before harvest time. Visiting preachers held services twice a day for a week. In passionate sermons they exhorted the congregation to turn away from sin and follow Jesus. During each service the preacher asked if anyone was ready to take Christ into his or her heart. Those who came forward were said to be "born

Jimmy Carter at a Future Farmers of America camp during his early teens.

again" as Christians and were expected to lead better lives. Baptists also put great stress on baptism, the rite of washing that made a child or adult a full member of the church. With his family's encouragement, Jimmy was baptized at the age of eleven.

In 1938, when Jimmy was 14, electrical power came to Plains and the surrounding towns. The Carter farmhouse got an electric light in every room, and even an electric refrigerator. Earl Carter was elected to the board of the Sumter Electric Membership Corporation, which determined where new power lines would run and set rates for customers. The whole community turned out for annual meetings of the corporation. Earl Carter made several trips to Washington, D.C., to talk to legislators about the needs of the rural South.

Electricity came to millions of small towns and farms in the late 1930s because of a program established by Democratic president Franklin D. Roosevelt. Jimmy's father, like most Georgians at the time, was a Democrat, and he was grateful for federal grants that made electricity possible in south Georgia. At the same time, however, he was deeply opposed to many of President Roosevelt's programs, which increased the power of the federal government. Earl Carter felt that the federal government was meddling in the business of southern farmers. Jimmy heard endless tirades against President Roosevelt at the dinner table.

The New Deal

During the 1930s, the United States sank into a disastrous economic depression. Factories closed, farmers lost their land, and millions of people lost their jobs and their homes.

In an effort to help the nation recover, President Franklin D. Roosevelt promoted a series of "back to work" programs as part of a plan called the New Deal. The government established programs to build new roads and public buildings and extend electricity to rural areas. Millions who had lost their jobs worked in these government programs.

During the Depression, the price of meat and produce fell so low that few farmers could earn a living. In an attempt to drive prices back up, the government paid farmers *not* to grow or sell certain crops. Even though they received government payments, many farmers resented having to plow their crops under and destroy their livestock. The idea of destroying crops and animals went against everything they knew and believed in.

☆ ☆ ☆

One of the memorable events of Jimmy's childhood was a huge rally for the re-election of Georgia's governor, Eugene Talmadge, in 1934. Some 30,000 people attended. Through the afternoon, bands played, vendors sold cold drinks and souvenirs, and everyone filled up on delicious barbecued pork. That night, the great Talmadge spoke to a wildly cheering crowd. This was ten-year-old Jimmy Carter's introduction to political campaigning, and it was a thrill he never forgot.

Georgia governor Eugene Talmadge was a powerful Southern Democrat who opposed the New Deal policies of Democratic president Franklin Roosevelt.

Classrooms and Playgrounds ──────────

Like all of the white children in the area, Jimmy Carter attended Plains High School, which combined elementary and high school grades under one roof. Three hundred pupils from first through eleventh grades (there was no twelfth grade) studied in the big brick building, its front entrance flanked by tall white columns. The classrooms were not wired for electricity. Each classroom had a wall of windows, and as long as the sun was shining, there was plenty of light. Until he reached seventh grade Jimmy went to school barefoot. He learned to walk with care on the splintery pine floorboards.

Though the Plains High School had limited resources, Jimmy Carter always felt that it gave him an excellent education. The school principal and English teacher, Miss Julia Coleman, was a dedicated educator who cared about each student. She tried to instill a love of learning and an appreciation for the arts in all of her pupils. Jimmy was one of her favorites. He already knew how to read when he entered first grade. He recalled that soon he was reading almost all the time, "on rainy days, Sunday afternoons, in bed at night, at the table during meals, in my tree house, on the toilet, and between and even during classes at school." After he exhausted the contents of the school library, Miss Julia brought him books from the county library in Americus. She was delighted when Jimmy read the immense novel *War and Peace*, by the Russian writer Leo Tolstoy, at the age of twelve. She

A formal portrait of high school student Jimmy Carter.

made a special announcement about his achievement during a school assembly. Miss Julia also taught students how to read aloud and deliver their own speeches.

Jimmy Carter was an excellent student, and he was full of confidence in the classroom. On the playground, however, he often felt timid and cautious. He was small for his age, and some of the bigger boys tried to bully him. He was quick and agile, and took part in sports where size didn't matter. On the playground he enjoyed playing marbles, spinning tops, and pitching horseshoes. Baseball was one of his favorite activities. Jimmy and his classmates played baseball before the morning school bell, during recess, and in the afternoons until the school bus came. One game could stretch over an entire week. By tenth grade Jimmy had grown tall enough to play varsity basketball. He was still the smallest member of the team, and acquired the nickname "Peewee."

Nearly all of the boys expected to become farmers like their fathers. They belonged to a national organization called the Future Farmers of America (FFA), which worked closely with the school to provide training in agricultural methods. Students took classes on raising crops and livestock. They learned to mend farm equipment and to shoe horses. Jimmy and his classmates raised calves and hogs, entering them in statewide competitions. Yet even though Jimmy was active in the FFA, he did not want to spend his life on the farm. Jimmy Carter dreamed of attending college. He wanted to see the world.

Chapter 2

Letters from Uncle Tom ——————

Most of Jimmy Carter's aunts, uncles, and cousins lived in or near Plains. Lillian Carter's brother, Tom Gordy, was the exception. As a young man, he had joined the United States Navy and made it his career. He sent letters home from all over the world describing his adventures. Whenever one of Uncle Tom's letters arrived, Jimmy wrote back with a barrage of questions. For years Jimmy and his uncle kept up a lively correspondence. When anyone asked Jimmy what he wanted to do when he grew up, he had his answer ready. He wanted to be a navy man.

From the beginning, Earl and Lillian Carter encouraged their son's ambition. They knew that Jimmy was very bright, and they believed he should continue his education beyond Plains High School. They realized, however, that they could not afford to send him to college. The U.S. Naval Academy, at Annapolis, Maryland, might offer a cost-free education and a career away from the farm. The big challenge would be gaining one of the widely coveted appointments to study there.

Appointments to the service academies were made only by U.S. senators and representatives. Earl Carter focused his attention on local congressman Stephen Pace. He contributed to Pace's campaigns. He introduced the congressman to Jimmy and showed him Jimmy's academic record. Yet when Jimmy graduated from high school in June 1941, Pace did not give him an appointment to the Naval Academy. Jimmy was still only 16 years old, and Pace suggested that he attend a nearby junior college to improve his qualifications for the academy. Carter entered Georgia Southwestern College in September 1941. The school was in the nearby town of Americus, and at first he lived at home. He was still consumed by his desire to enter the navy, and he took courses that filled in gaps in his high school record.

On Sunday morning, December 7, 1941, shocking news swept the United States. Japanese bombers had attacked the U.S. naval fleet at Pearl Harbor, in Hawaii. The next day, the nation declared war on Japan, entering World War II. Now Jimmy Carter was even more determined to enter the Naval Academy. It was his ambition to command a submarine.

In the spring of 1942, Jimmy completed his year at Southwestern. Earl Carter pressed Congressman Pace for an appointment to the Naval Academy. This

The USS *Arizona* burns after the Japanese attack on Pearl Harbor, Hawaii, on December 7, 1941. The *Tennessee* and the *Virginia* at left have also been hit.

time Pace promised to make the appointment if Jimmy would study for one more year at the Georgia Institute of Technology, where he could take advanced math and science courses required by the academy. Jimmy moved away from home for the first time, living and studying in Atlanta, the biggest city in the South.

Representative Pace kept his word, and in the spring of 1943, he nominated Jimmy Carter for an appointment to the Naval Academy. That June, Jimmy Carter boarded a train to Washington, D.C., then took a bus to Annapolis. At last he was officially admitted to the U.S. Naval Academy. He was two years out of Plains High School, but he was still only 18 years old.

Reveille and Romance

For an entering student at the Naval Academy, life was strictly regimented. The students, known as midshipmen, awakened at six in the morning to a bugle playing "Reveille." The days were tightly scheduled with classes, drills, and study periods until lights-out at ten in the evening. Midshipmen had almost no time to themselves.

Midshipman Jimmy Carter ate, studied, and lived with the hundred men of his company. He soon learned that upperclassmen hazed new students relentlessly. They forced the new midshipmen to do countless push-ups and run obstacle courses in the dark. The new recruits were ordered to research obscure topics at the library and to deliver long recitations in the mess hall. Because Carter came

The U.S. Naval Academy at Annapolis is one of four training colleges for U.S. military officers. The others are the U.S. Military Academy at West Point, New York; the Air Force Academy at Colorado Springs, Colorado; and the Coast Guard Academy at New London, Connecticut. The Naval Academy was founded in 1845. Students enroll for a four-year course of study which includes rigorous academic classes and practical training on naval vessels.

☆ ☆ ☆

from the South, his tormentors ordered him to sing the Civil War song "Marching Through Georgia," in which Yankee soldiers boast of their victorious trek across the state. Carter refused to sing it, accepting a painful paddling instead. In August Carter wrote in his diary, "Over five months to Christmas! I hope I can stand it!"

As the hazing let up, Carter found that the Naval Academy was everything he hoped it would be. He did well in his classes and made many close friends. He also took part in athletics, running cross-country and playing football on the team for players under 140 pounds (64 kilograms). During the summer of 1944, he had his first direct experience sailing on a naval vessel, the USS *New York*. German submarines were prowling along U.S. shores, and on one occasion the *New York* limped back to port with a damaged propeller, perhaps the result of a German torpedo.

While he was at Annapolis, Carter maintained close ties to his family back home. He wrote regularly to his parents and sisters. One day his sister Ruth showed Carter's picture to one of her friends, Rosalynn Smith. Rosalynn, nearly three years younger than Jimmy, was intrigued by the handsome young man in his midshipman's uniform. The next time Carter was home for a short vacation, Ruth introduced him to Rosalynn. Jimmy was enchanted by a young woman who seemed shy and self-assured at the same time. He asked her for a date. When he returned home that night he announced to his mother, "She's the girl I'm going to marry."

Earl and Lillian Carter had mixed feeling about their son's romance. They knew and liked Rosalynn, but had hoped that Jimmy could find a more sophisticated girl from somewhere else. Meanwhile, Rosalynn had her doubts about Jimmy. When he urged that they get married right away, she resisted. He finally

Rosalynn

Eleanor Rosalynn Smith was born on August 18, 1927, and grew up in Plains. Her father was an auto repairman who did odd jobs and managed a small farm. When Rosalynn was 13, her father died of leukemia. Before his death he urged his children to go to college. Rosalynn did her best to follow his advice. She graduated from Plains High School as valedictorian of her class in 1944, then went to Georgia Southwestern, the two-year college in nearby Americus. Through her life she placed a high value on education.

☆ ★ ☆

Jimmy's mother and fiancée pin on the bars that identify him as an ensign after his graduation from the U.S. Naval Academy.

persuaded her. Jimmy Carter and Rosalynn Smith were married in Plains on July 7, 1946, shortly after he graduated from the Naval Academy. He was a few months shy of 22 and Rosalynn would turn 19 in August. Shortly before the wedding Jimmy gave Rosalynn a book called *The Navy Wife*. The book was filled with advice for women married to naval officers. Rosalynn studied the book devotedly, but it little prepared her for the life that lay ahead.

Jimmy and Rosalynn on their wedding day in July 1946.

Under the Sea

Carter's class at the Naval Academy had to finish its studies in three years instead of the usual four because the United States was at war and expected to need new naval officers desperately. In 1945, however, both Germany and Japan surrendered to Allied forces, ending World War II. When Carter graduated in June 1946, he entered a rapidly shrinking peacetime navy.

Carter still hoped to command a submarine someday. Before he would be accepted to a submarine post, he first had to serve two years on a surface vessel. He was assigned to the USS *Wyoming*, a crumbling old battleship harbored at Norfolk, Virginia. Carter spent four days a week and one of his three "off" nights on shipboard. Rosalynn lived in an apartment in Norfolk, awaiting Carter's return from his four- and five-day absences. In July 1947, their first son, Jack, was born. Rosalynn had few friends in Norfolk, and she was often lonely. She felt overwhelmed by the responsibility of caring for a tiny baby all by herself. She quickly discovered that complaining to her husband was useless. "He had and still has no patience with tears," she wrote later, "thinking instead that one makes the best of whatever situation, and with a smile."

In 1947 the *Wyoming* was *decommissioned* (retired from service), and Carter was reassigned to the USS *Mississippi*, another battleship stationed in

Ensign Carter was first assigned to the USS *Wyoming*, an aging battleship.

★ TO SEE THE WORLD ★

The Carter Children

Jimmy and Rosalynn Carter had three sons and a daughter. Jack was born in 1947, Chip in 1950, and Jeff in 1952. By the time their father was elected president, all three were adults. Amy was born in 1967; she was nine years old when her father took office and spent the next four years in the White House.

☆ ★ ☆

Norfolk. Finally, in June 1948, Carter was assigned to a six-month training program for submarine officers in New London, Connecticut. The course was very demanding, with hands-on training as well as formal lectures. Carter graduated third in his class of 52. He was assigned to the USS *Pomfret*, a submarine based in Honolulu, Hawaii. Days after Carter arrived, the *Pomfret* set off on a three-month cruise across the Pacific to the coast of China. Rosalynn and baby Jack stayed in Plains until Jimmy returned to port.

Carter served in a variety of posts on the *Pomfret*, including electronics officer. When he wasn't on duty, he spent most of his time studying manuals and troubleshooting equipment. "Jimmy was not one of the guys," a fellow officer remembered. "We didn't criticize him or anything, because he was an incredibly determined and responsible officer. But he was always apart. He never really got close to anybody."

When Carter returned to Honolulu, he was reunited with his young family. They had a few months to enjoy Hawaii, then moved with the *Pomfret* to a new assignment in San Diego, California, where they lived for 18 months. In February 1951, Carter was reassigned once to Groton, Connecticut. There he participated in the final preparations of a new submarine, the USS *K-1*, the first U.S. submarine built since the war ended. When the *K-1* was commissioned in November, Carter became part of its crew, serving at different times as executive officer, engineering officer, and electronics repair officer.

In 1952 Lieutenant Carter applied to train under Captain Hyman Rickover on a new kind of submarine, a vessel fueled by nuclear power. Rickover interviewed Carter for more than two hours, firing questions at him on everything from art to military history. Finally he inquired about Carter's studies at the Naval Academy: "Did you do your best?" he asked. Carter recalled his answer years later:

> I recalled several of the many times at the Academy when I could have learned more. . . . I finally gulped and said, "No sir, I didn't *always* do my best." He looked at me for a long time. Then . . . he asked one final question, which I've never been able to forget, or to answer. He said, "Why not?"

Carter and Admiral Hyman Rickover (right), the "father of the nuclear submarine," visiting a sub during Carter's presidency.

Carter was accepted into the nuclear submarine program. Late in 1952 he and the family moved again, first to Schenectady, New York, then to Washington, D.C. There Carter was assigned to the U.S. Atomic Energy Commission, which was working with the General Electric Company to build the nuclear power plant for the submarine *Seawolf*.

Meanwhile, back in Georgia, Earl Carter had been elected to a seat in the state *legislature* (the state's lawmaking body). Then, early in 1953, he was diagnosed with cancer and given only a few months to live. Jimmy rushed back to Plains to be at his father's bedside. They filled their days with deep conversations about family history, business, and life. Jimmy Carter was awed by the stream of friends, both black and white, who came to bid his father farewell.

Shortly before Earl Carter died, Jimmy's mother asked him to come home and run the family farm. Carter had been away for eleven years. Now it was time for him to return to Plains.

Chapter 3

Back to the Land

After his father's funeral, Jimmy Carter had a long talk with Rosalynn. He told her he had decided to leave the navy. He wanted go back to Georgia and run the family farm. Rosalynn was horrified. Jimmy had a promising career as a naval officer. How could he give up everything he had worked so hard to achieve? And how could he condemn her and their children to life in rural Georgia? After her years away, she felt that Plains had almost nothing to offer them. The town didn't have a library or a kindergarten program. There wasn't even a pool where they could swim on hot days.

Carter had made up his mind, however, and she could not dissuade him. He wanted to follow his father's example, to have a positive impact on the lives of humble farmers and townspeople. Furthermore, his work with the military had begun to clash with his religious beliefs. Years later he explained that he believed "God did not intend me to spend my life working on instruments of destruction to kill people." In October 1953, James Earl Carter was honorably discharged from the U.S. Navy.

Carter returned to the farm at a difficult time. Even though the family had 5,000 acres (2,025 ha) of valuable land, a severe drought had struck the region, reducing crop yields. Worse, local farmers who had borrowed money from the Carters to farm the land couldn't repay their loans. The Carter businesses were short of cash.

Between tending the fields and the family's farm supply store, Carter worked 16- to 18-hour days. Rosalynn ably handled the bookkeeping and accounting. Eager to learn about new agricultural methods, Carter pored over books and journals at night. He threw himself into farming with the same determination he had shown in the navy.

By 1955 the drought had abated and the Carter farm turned a healthy profit. As his financial worries faded, Carter found time to get involved in civic activities. He joined the Lions Club and headed the Community Development Committee. He helped establish a new medical clinic in Plains. One of Carter's pet projects was to get a new public swimming pool built. Following the racial code that still ruled the South, the new pool was open only to the town's white citizens.

After his return to Georgia, Jimmy Carter shovels peanuts on the family farm.

Segregation faced a ringing challenge in May 1954 from the U.S. Supreme Court. In a landmark case called *Brown* v. *Board of Education of Topeka*, the court ruled that supposedly "separate but equal" schools were not really equal. Such schools violated the U.S. Constitution, the court wrote, because they did not give African American students equal treatment under the law. It ordered that public schools be *integrated*, allowing students of different races to attend the same schools and receive the same education.

In Plains, and throughout the South, the ruling angered and frightened most white people. At first Carter did not take a firm stand on one side or the other. When he heard the decision and the angry responses, he was worried. "I don't know what's going to happen around here," he said to Rosalynn.

Encouraged by the Supreme Court decision, civil-rights activists continued to press for change. In 1955 a black woman in Montgomery, Alabama, refused to move to the blacks-only section of a bus and was arrested. Soon African Americans there, led by local pastor Martin Luther King Jr., organized a *boycott*, refusing to ride the buses or shop in white-owned stores until the law was changed. Later, African American students "sat in" at lunch counters in local stores, defying segregation in eating establishments. In 1961 two African American students enrolled at the University of Georgia, where no black person had ever been admitted.

White groups in the South were determined to resist integration. In many towns, White Citizens Councils were formed to encourage resistance among whites and to intimidate and threaten African Americans. One day in Plains, several members of the local council appeared at the Carter store. They grimly pointed out to Carter that he was the only white man in Plains who was not a member of the group. The men warned Carter that his refusal to join could hurt his business. Carter was worried, but he refused to join. As one friend remembered, "You knew Jimmy was a person who had no truck with that kind of stuff. . . . You did not have to sit down and talk with him, you just knew it."

Running for Office

In 1961 the Carters moved into a brick ranch-style house near the center of Plains. They were among the most prosperous families in Sumter County. Both of them had grown up in Plains, but their neighbors sometimes saw them as outsiders. Their years in the wider world during Carter's navy service had made them different.

With the family business prospering, Jimmy Carter began to feel confined in Plains. He looked for a wider field of action. In 1962 he found it. That fall the Georgia government announced a change in election procedures for the state senate and called special elections to fill vacant seats. Carter announced that he would run for the Democratic nomination for the senate from his local district. At the time, nearly all Georgians were Democrats, so winning the Democratic *primary election* usually meant being elected to the office.

Carter threw himself into the campaign with his usual zeal. In the summer of 1962 he traveled tirelessly throughout the seven counties of the senate district.

A poster for Jimmy Carter's first political campaign. After winning a disputed primary election, Carter won the a seat in the Georgia state senate in November 1962.

He was not a strong public speaker, but when he talked to people in small groups, he was highly persuasive. On the campaign trail he talked to farmers, preachers, homemakers, and storekeepers. He spoke about helping create a new and more forward-looking Georgia.

On the day of the primary, Carter drove from county to county, trying to gauge how the election was going. He sensed that he was doing well in most parts of the district. Then he visited Georgetown, the seat of Quitman County. Years later he described what he discovered: "Campaign cards of my opponent were on the voting table, and the [county] supervisor would point to the cards and say to each voter, 'This is a good man, and he's my friend.' He would watch the ballot being marked and then dropped into a hole in the top of a large pasteboard box, and on several occasions he reached into the box and extracted a few ballots to be examined. . . . He completely ignored my protests. All the other poll workers seemed to obey his orders."

When the votes were tallied at the end of the day, Carter's opponent, Homer Moore, had won the election, thanks to his lopsided victory in Quitman County. Carter protested the election irregularities to Democratic officials. When they would not act, he took his case to a newspaper. John Pennington, a reporter with the *Atlanta Journal*, uncovered a long history of vote fraud in Quitman County. In a series of front-page stories, he revealed that dead people, prisoners, and people who no longer lived in Georgia were listed as registered voters in Quitman County and had cast ballots in one election after another. In the race for state senate, 333 voters had voted in the county, but election officials counted more than 400 ballots, 360 of them for Carter's opponent.

An Atlanta lawyer, Charles Kirbo, agreed to take Carter's case to court. On November 2, a judge threw out votes from Quitman County because of major irregularities in the voting. Without those votes, Jimmy Carter won the Democratic nomination after all. In the general election four days after the judge's decision, he sailed to victory over a Republican candidate.

To the Governor's Mansion

By the time he took office, Carter was ready for his new challenge as a state senator. He took a speed-reading course to help him get through the mountains of mail, proposed bills, and other paperwork. He was especially interested in education issues and ways to cut government waste. In 1964 he helped pass a bill on election reform.

Politics was Carter's new passion. He left the farm and the store largely in the hands of his brother Billy, and he began considering his next campaign for office. In 1966 he announced that he would run for a seat in the U.S. House of Representatives. The congressional seat in Carter's district was held by Howard H. Callaway, the first Republican elected to Congress in Georgia since the 1870s. A popular figure in the district, Callaway seemed unbeatable to many, but Carter looked forward to the challenge of running against him.

Then Callaway made a surprise announcement. Instead of running for Congress again, he declared, he would run for governor. Without Callaway as his opponent, Carter was almost certain to win the congressional seat. However, the race had lost much of its excitement for Carter. He wanted to take on Callaway, so he announced that he too would run for governor.

Winning the governorship was a tall order. Before he faced Callaway, Carter first had to win the Democratic primary against a strong field of well-known state leaders. Carter worked ceaselessly, but in the end, he finished third. In a runoff between the two top candidates, conservative Democrat Lester Maddox won. The loser, Ellis Arnall, refused to give up, however. In the general election he ran as a write-in candidate. Once again no candidate won a majority of the vote. The election was decided by the state legislature. Even though Callaway had the most votes, the Democratic majority declared Lester Maddox the next governor.

The unsuccessful run for the governor's seat left Carter weary and discouraged. His spirits lifted with the birth of his daughter Amy in 1967. Another crucial factor was his renewed commitment to his religious beliefs. Through long hours of Bible study and prayer, Carter deepened and strengthened his faith. "I formed a much more intimate relationship with Christ," he wrote later. "Since then I've had a new life."

Supported by his family and his faith, Carter made up his mind to run for governor again in 1970. This time he was determined to win. In 1966 many Georgians saw Carter as a liberal Democrat, a champion of integrated schools, and an enemy of White Citizens Councils. As he prepared for the 1970 race, Carter was careful to appeal to Georgia's conservative voters. He promised to return control of the schools to local authorities. This strongly suggested that he would support white families who wanted their children to attend all-white schools. His campaign strategy proved successful. In September 1970, he won the Democratic primary, and in November he won the general election. On January 12, 1971, he was inaugurated governor of the state of Georgia.

Chapter 4

A New Voice from the Old South ———

Conservatives in Georgia had supported Jimmy Carter because they believed he would defend the old rules of racial segregation. When he took office in January 1971, however, his inaugural address set a very different tone. "I say to you quite frankly that the time for racial discrimination is over," he declared. "No poor, rural, weak, or black person should ever have to bear the additional burden of being deprived of the opportunity of an education, a job, or simple justice."

Carter's speech lasted only twelve minutes, but it left a powerful impression. The *New York Times* ran a story about Georgia's new governor the next morning. *Time* magazine ranked Carter as one of the "new voices" of the South. In Georgia, liberals and African Americans praised his speech and waited eagerly to see what he would do as governor. Conservatives, on the other hand, felt betrayed.

Carter delivers his inaugural address as governor of Georgia on January 12, 1971. Seated at right is lieutenant governor Lester Maddox.

One of Carter's fiercest opponents was outgoing governor Lester Maddox. State law kept Maddox from running again for governor so he had gained election as lieutenant governor, the second-highest executive position in the state. An outspoken opponent of school desegregation, Lieutenant Governor Maddox often worked to undermine measures supported by Governor Carter.

In Carter's position, a different politician would have looked for ways to swap favors with his conservative opponents to gain support for his own program. Carter detested such deals, however, and never developed much skill in that sort of political maneuver. When legislators approached him about making such compromises, his reaction was often angry. Once he exclaimed to one of his aides, "If one more legislator walks through that door and asks for some trade-off deal, so help me God, I think I'll throttle him!"

Still, Carter had a broad base of support, and he made many positive changes during his term. He worked for environmental protection, reform of the judicial system, and improvement of the public schools. With Rosalynn's encouragement, he placed mental-health services among his leading concerns. While he was in office, Georgia opened 111 community mental-health centers around the state.

One of Carter's most absorbing projects was an attempt to reorganize the state government. He was convinced that Georgia could save billions of dollars if its government were streamlined. Carter and his staff designed a plan for consolidating

Carter testifies before a congressional committee in Washington, D.C., during his term as governor.

scores of small, inefficient agencies, bureaus, and departments into larger groupings that would be more effective. He faced strong opposition, however, and only parts of his reorganization project were implemented.

In keeping with his inaugural promise, Carter opened job opportunities for African Americans at every level of state government. Carter also showed his support of the black community by honoring the Georgia-born civil-rights leader Dr. Martin Luther King Jr., who had been assassinated in 1968. In January 1973, he issued a public pronouncement honoring King's birthday. The following year he placed a portrait of King in the rotunda of the state capitol. King's widow, Coretta Scott King, unveiled the portrait. King's father, the Reverend Martin Luther King Sr., a widely respected pastor in Atlanta, said Carter was "one of the finest men I ever met."

Carter enjoyed being governor. He thrived on finding ways to solve the state's problems and dealing with people from every corner of Georgia. As time passed, however, he began to think about his next step. The Georgia constitution would not allow him to run for re-election in 1974, and he hungered for an even greater challenge.

As governor, Carter met many of the country's leading Democrats, including several Democratic presidential candidates. Much as he admired them, he concluded that he was as intelligent as they, and he believed that he was more disciplined. He began planning a run for the presidency.

In 1972 the Democratic presidential nominee, George McGovern, was badly defeated by President Richard Nixon. Even as that Democratic campaign

president if Ford promised to pardon him later on. By pardoning Nixon, Ford caused the public to question his own honesty.

"Why Not the Best?"

Meanwhile, in June 1973, Jimmy Carter was appointed chairman of the 1974 Democratic campaign, responsible for national strategy in Democratic efforts to elect more representatives and senators in the off-year elections. In this role he traveled the country, meeting ordinary voters and Democratic leaders in most of the key states. More and more people knew his name and saw him as a strength in the party. In November, Democrats made huge gains in the elections, winning 49 new seats in the House and 4 seats in the Senate. The main reason for the victory was popular outrage over Watergate, but campaign chairman Carter could take some of the credit.

In December 1974, only weeks after the successful election, Jimmy Carter announced his decision to run for the 1976 Democratic nomination. Carter declared that a crisis of public confidence gripped the nation. He said that the American people deserved an honest president. "I will never lie to you," he promised. He added, "It is now time to stop and ask ourselves the question which my last commanding officer, Admiral Hyman Rickover, asked me. . . . For our nation, and for all of us, that question is: Why not the best?" Rickover's question became the motto of the Carter campaign.

In December 1974, Jimmy Carter announces that he will seek the Democratic nomination for president in 1976.

During 1975 Carter courted the public. As he wrote later, "Our strategy was simple—make a total effort all over the country." He portrayed himself as a solid moderate candidate. He was closer to the political center than most other Democrats seeking the nomination. More important, he was better organized and better prepared for the campaign.

By early 1976, Carter was ready for the Democratic primary elections. Unlike many candidates, he waged a national campaign, entering all but four state primaries. He won the New Hampshire primary, the first of the year, and later showed special strength in the South. When the Democratic convention met in New York City in July, Carter had won enough supporters in the primaries to win the nomination on the first ballot. As his running mate he chose Senator Walter Mondale of Minnesota. Carter's determination had paid off once again.

Meanwhile, President Ford received an unexpected challenge from within the Republican party. Former California governor Ronald Reagan, a leader of the party's conservatives, gained an enthusiastic following and ran against Ford in a number of primaries. Although Ford overcame Reagan's challenge and won the nomination, the Republican party was left with deep divisions.

The Race to the White House

Jimmy Carter had no personal experience dealing with issues beyond those of Georgia. He had never served in Washington as an elected or appointed official. Ordinarily, such inexperience would be a serious disadvantage. In 1976, however, Carter turned his outsider status into a major asset. In the shadow of the Watergate scandals and Ford's pardon of a discredited president, many voters were looking for a new start. With no connection to Washington politics, Carter could run as a

Carter's presidential campaign headquarters in Plains, Georgia, in a former train depot.

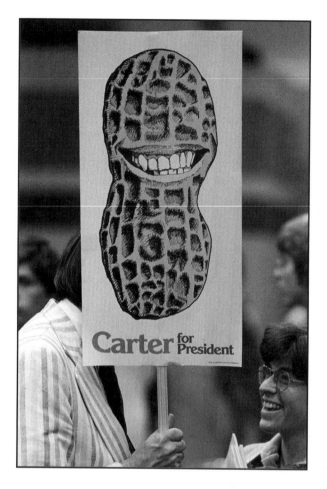

A Carter campaign sign featuring a peanut and the candidate's famous grin.

true outsider, promising to begin a new era of honesty in government. As one reporter put it, "Jimmy was a stranger in town. They had no reason to distrust him, and he didn't give them one."

While campaigning during the sweltering summer months, Carter took time to learn as much as he could about major issues facing the country. He invited a stream of economists, political scientists, and foreign-policy experts to visit Plains. There he plied them with questions and listened to their answers with keen attention. Most of these experts were amazed by Carter's quick grasp of the issues.

Carter continued to court the votes of both liberals and conservatives. Lest he offend one group or the other, he avoided making strong statements about what he would do if elected. President Ford seized every opportunity to accuse Carter of being indecisive.

"He wavers, he wanders, he wiggles, and he waffles," Ford said, "and he shouldn't be president of the United States." Carter's mediocre abilities as a public speaker drew fire from reporters. One journalist claimed he was "allergic to all efforts at eloquence."

In nationwide polls of registered voters, Ford and Carter remained extremely close throughout the summer. Then in September, Carter made a serious blunder. In an interview with *Playboy* magazine, he said he had always been faithful to his wife, but then confessed that he had "looked on a lot of women with lust" and "committed adultery in [his] heart many times." Some voters were scandalized, while others were embarrassed by the personal nature of the confession. Carter tumbled in the polls, and Ford took a promising lead.

The Man from Michigan

President Gerald Ford grew up in Grand Rapids, Michigan. An outstanding athlete, he won a football scholarship to the University of Michigan. He earned a law degree from Yale University Law School and served in World War II. He returned to Grand Rapids and soon was elected to the U.S. House of Representatives, where he served for 25 years, becoming the leader of the Republican minority. Ford was chosen to be vice president by President Nixon because of his unblemished record for honesty and his loyalty to the party. As president, Ford worked diligently to end the "national nightmare" of Watergate and rebuild the citizens' trust in the presidency.

☆★☆

Jimmy, Rosalynn, and nine-year-old Amy Carter accept the cheers of the crowd in November 1976 after Carter's election victory over Gerald Ford.

Then it was Ford's turn to make a mistake. That fall Ford and Carter met for three televised debates. During the second debate, watched by some 100 million viewers, Ford stated, "There is no Soviet domination of Eastern Europe, and there never will be under a Ford administration." Most viewers knew that Eastern Europe had been under Soviet control since the late 1940s. Ford later said he had meant to say that the countries of Eastern Europe had never *accepted* Soviet control, but he could not erase the impression that he did not know simple facts about foreign affairs. His ratings plunged, while Carter's rose once more.

On the night of the election, Carter waited with Rosalynn at their Atlanta headquarters. The vote was breathtakingly close. Finally, at 3:30 in the morning, it became clear that Carter would win the election. He received 40.8 million popular votes, 50.1 percent of the total, to Ford's 39.1 million, or 48 percent. In the electoral college, Carter received 297 electoral votes to Ford's 240.

James Earl Carter, the boy from Plains, would be the 39th president of the United States.

Chapter 5

Smooth Roads and Rough

On January 20, 1977, Jimmy Carter delivered a brief inaugural address from the east portico of the Capitol. After past inaugurations, the president had ridden along Pennsylvania Avenue to the White House in a horse-drawn carriage or a limousine. Carter broke with this tradition. Hand in hand with Rosalynn, he walked the mile and a half (2.4 km). The gesture delighted the public. Carter had promised a presidency more closely in touch with the people, and already he was fulfilling his pledge.

Once inside the White House, Carter asked the Secret Service staff to lead the way to the Oval Office. There he requested to be left alone. In awe he surveyed the room where earlier presidents had made decisions that changed the world. In the coming years, he too would be called upon to make world-shaping choices.

In the inaugural parade, Jimmy and Rosalynn Carter become the first president and first lady to walk from the Capitol Building to the White House. Earlier presidents rode in horse-drawn carriages or open cars.

Jimmy Carter had always sought out challenges. Now he faced the greatest challenge of his lifetime.

On his first full day in office he signed an executive order granting *amnesty*, or pardon, to thousands of young men who left the United States during the Vietnam War. Most had gone to Canada or Europe to avoid being drafted into the military during the war. Under the amnesty they could return home without danger of arrest. President Ford had urged that these draft resisters be treated with leniency, but he and most other Republicans opposed amnesty. Senator Barry Goldwater of Arizona declared that the amnesty was "the most disgraceful thing a president has ever done." To Carter and his supporters, however, it was an act of forgiveness and reconciliation.

Carter appointed Georgians to a number of high positions in his administration. Among them was Bert Lance, a Georgia businessman and a close friend, who was appointed to head the Office of Management and Budget (OMB). Hamilton Jordan and Jody Powell, who had helped coordinate Carter's presidential campaign, held key positions. Jordan served as White House chief of staff and Powell served as press secretary. Though they were young and lacked experience in the capital, they were loyal and intelligent. Carter placed great trust in them.

"Everybody has warned me not to take on too many projects so early in the administration," Carter wrote in his diary during his second week as president. Yet

President Carter and his mother, Miss Lillian, in the White House. After working for many years as a nurse, she joined the Peace Corps at age 68 and served as a medical aide in India.

he felt compelled to attack every problem he saw. During his first six months in the White House he proposed a deluge of new laws and programs. He pushed to create two new federal departments, dealing with energy and consumer affairs. He called for welfare reform, tax reform, control of health-care costs, and changes in the Social Security system. As he had done in Georgia, he launched plans to reorganize and scale down the federal government.

Carter had campaigned on the promise that he would balance the federal budget. Now that he was in office, he tried to trim costs he considered unnecessary. President Ford had authorized the construction of more than 300 dams on U.S. rivers. After reviewing the plans, Carter decided that most of the dams were not needed. He cut the authorization for all but 19 of the dams, with a proposed saving of $5.1 billion. Many members of Congress were furious at the cuts. The dam projects had been designed to create needed jobs and business opportunities in their home districts. Carter had not consulted Congress before announcing the cuts. Instead, he simply pressed ahead with his own agenda.

The incident was an example of Carter's tendency to act on his own. Some members of Congress tried to teach him the ways of Capitol Hill. Speaker Thomas "Tip" O'Neill, the most powerful Democrat in the House of Representatives, wrote, "I tried to explain how important it was for the president to work

President Carter meets with Speaker of the House Thomas "Tip" O'Neill.

closely with the Congress. He didn't seem to understand." Robert Byrd, a power-ful Democratic senator from West Virginia, warned Carter, "The road can be smooth or the road can be rough." By the summer of 1977, it was clear that some rough roads lay ahead.

A Sea of Troubles

In the summer of 1977, Congress approved establishing the new Department of Energy. Carter nominated James Schlesinger to serve as its first secretary. Carter was deeply concerned about the nation's increasing dependence on foreign oil. He designed a package of new energy bills intended to cut down on U.S. energy consumption. These included a tax on large "gas-guzzling" automobiles and tax credits for businesses that conserved energy. Carter also championed the development of solar power and other energy sources not requiring fossil fuel. The proposals were supported strongly by environmental groups, but they faced determined opposition from auto manufacturers and energy companies. The measures moved slowly through Congress, tugged, sliced, and twisted by supporters and opponents. By the time they passed in October 1978, many had been seriously weakened.

In the case of welfare reform, Carter was unhappy with the system as it existed and wanted to reform it. Yet he insisted that the reforms be accomplished without increasing government spending. This proved to be all but impossible. These mixed signals encouraged those in Congress who opposed Carter's reforms. After months of debate and reams of paperwork, no substantial changes came about.

In the summer of 1977, news broke that Carter's Georgia friend Bert Lance was under investigation for fraudulent banking practices. Lance was accused of using his influence as head of the Office of Management and Budget to obtain a loan of $3.4 million from the National Bank of Chicago. Carter had campaigned on the pledge that he would build an honest government in the wake of Watergate. Now one of his most trusted appointees was in danger of indictment. At first Carter tried to defend Lance, but later he asked him to resign. Bert Lance resigned on September 21, 1977.

☆ ★ ☆

A *Time* magazine cover shows Carter's disgraced budget director Bert Lance as Humpty Dumpty. Carter is shown as one of "the king's men" who "couldn't put Humpty together again."

World Affairs

Carter was floundering on the domestic front. At first, he fared little better in the dizzying world of international relations. He vowed that he would take a strong stand on human rights, stating that the United States would not tolerate human-rights abuses anywhere on the globe. A special target was the Soviet Union, America's long-standing rival as a world superpower. (The Soviet Union consisted of present-day Russia and 15 neighboring states that are now smaller independent countries.) Early in 1977, the State Department accused the Soviet Union of human-rights violations toward political *dissidents*, citizens who were protesting Soviet government policies. In response to this accusation, the Soviets took even more repressive measures toward dissidents. Tension between the two nations increased. For a time the Soviets broke off discussions on the critical issue of arms control.

Carter had more success in one of the most explosive regions on Earth, the Middle East. There conflict between the Jewish state of Israel and its Muslim neighbors had been going on for nearly 30 years. During and after World War II, thousands of Jewish emigrants and refugees settled in Palestine, displacing many Palestinians in the region. In 1947 the United Nations partitioned Palestine into Arab and Jewish regions, and in 1948, the Jewish region declared itself the independent state of Israel. Palestinians and their neighbors refused to accept the existence of Israel and vowed to take their lands back. Israel, surrounded by potential enemies, began to build Jewish settlements in Palestinian territories. After nearly 30 years the region still simmered with threats of violence.

Carter worked actively to help negotiate peace in the Middle East. He made repeated efforts to bring Israel and its neighbors together for a peace conference in Geneva, Switzerland. Time after time these efforts were rebuffed. Finally, Carter persuaded Egypt's president, Anwar al-Sadat, and Israel's prime minister, Menachem Begin, to come to the United States for talks at Camp David, the presidential retreat in Maryland. These face-to-face meetings by heads of state were highly unusual. Peace proposals are usually worked out quietly by low-level diplomats, then approved by national leaders.

The Camp David talks went on from September 5 to September 17, 1978. President Carter himself served as *mediator* (go-between) through 13 tension-filled days. During the process, these three very different men developed a close working relationship. In the end, Begin and Sadat signed two very significant documents. The first outlined a "framework for peace" in the region. The second was a treaty of peace between Egypt and Israel. Egypt became the first Muslim neighbor of Israel to recognize the Jewish state.

Most historians regard the Camp David Accords as the greatest achievement of Jimmy Carter's presidency. Begin and Sadat were awarded the 1978

President Carter with Egyptian president Anwar al-Sadat (left) and Israeli prime minister Menachem Begin after the signing of the Camp David Accords in September 1978. The agreement, bringing peace between Egypt and Israel, was one of Carter's great accomplishments as president.

Nobel Peace Prize for their efforts. They returned to Washington in March 1979 to sign the formal peace treaty between their countries at the White House. This event proved to be a high point of Carter's presidency.

The Shadow of Iran

Meanwhile, in another part of the Middle East, trouble was brewing. A revolution in Iran would prove to be the undoing of the Carter presidency. For years, the United States had supported the Iranian government led by the Shah of Iran, a kinglike leader who favored developing the country with the help of Western governments and businesses. Carter had visited the Shah on New Year's Eve in 1977, describing him as "an island of stability in one of the more troubled areas of the world."

The Shah of Iran, a United States ally, made a state visit to Washington in 1977. From the right, President Carter, the Shah, Rosalynn Carter, and the Shah's wife.

Other forces in Iran, especially Muslim religious leaders, opposed the Shah's policies. Beginning in 1978, they supported huge demonstrations against the Shah, urging that he be forced to give up his hereditary power. Finally, in January 1978, the Shah and his family left the country. The Shah's opponents celebrated in the streets. On February 1, the Ayatollah Khomeini, leader of the Muslim fundamentalists, announced the formation of a new Muslim government. Khomeini viewed the United States with distrust and hostility. American officials feared he would damage U.S. political, military, and business interests in the Middle East.

"A Crisis of Confidence"

In June 1978, President Carter traveled to Vienna to meet with Soviet premier Leonid Brezhnev. For years, the United States and the Soviet Union had been negotiating a second Strategic Arms Limitation Treaty (known as SALT II). Carter and Brezhnev had agreed on the final points, and on June 18, they signed the agreement. This appeared to be another international triumph for Jimmy Carter.

All was not well at home, however. Members of the major oil-producing nations had agreed to increase oil prices, and the price of gasoline soared to historic highs. Truckers led protests against the high prices, and in some regions gas supplies were scarce, causing long lines at the gas pumps. The spiraling cost of fuel was leading to many other price increases. The Carter administration seemed unable to deal with this growing problem.

Carter went to Camp David, the presidential retreat outside Washington, to consider his next steps. After discussing the country's problems with a wide range of Americans, he addressed the nation on July 15. In his speech, he said that the United States was facing a "crisis of confidence." He urged Americans to pull together and proposed a sweeping program to limit imports of foreign oil and to reduce energy consumption in the United States. At first, reaction to the speech was positive. On further thought, people concluded that Carter was too gloomy and preachy. He was the one who seemed overwhelmed by the country's problems. Their confidence in Carter's leadership continued its downward spiral.

Taken Hostage

The former Shah of Iran was a man without a country. In 1979 he learned he was seriously ill with cancer. In October, President Carter gave the Shah special permission to enter the United States for medical treatment. That action caused violent protests in Tehran, Iran's capital. On November 4, a band of Iranian revolutionaries seized the U.S. Embassy and took 66 Americans hostage. In the coming months they released 14 of the hostages, but they held the remaining 52, demanding that the Shah be returned to Iran to stand trial for abuses of power. Carter agonized over the fate of the hostages but refused the captors' demands.

The Iran hostage crisis became a story that would dominate the news for more than a year. Television reporters interviewed the distraught families and reported every day on their status. They began counting the days the hostages had

Islamic militants in front of the U.S. Embassy in Tehran, Iran, burn the Shah in effigy during a violent demonstration. They took over the embassy and held dozens of U.S. embassy workers hostage there for more than a year.

been in captivity. Carter was in a difficult position. He believed that returning the Shah—who would likely be put to death—was out of the question. Giving in to the kidnappers' demands would also encourage further kidnappings. Instead, Carter and his staff tried to negotiate with the kidnappers and with the new Iranian government. Month after month passed without progress. The American public watched and waited in dismay.

Just when it seemed that the world picture could get no worse, it did. On December 25, Soviet troops began to invade Afghanistan, which shared a long border with Iran. The Soviets had long influenced the Afghan government, but had recently lost power to local Muslim leaders. They invaded to regain their influence in Afghanistan and in the Middle East. Americans, brought up to fear and distrust the Soviet Union, were deeply concerned. Did this mark a turning point in the long Cold War between the United States and the Soviets? They also wondered why the invasion caught the U.S. government by surprise.

In January 1980, to show his displeasure with the Soviet invasion, President Carter asked the U.S. Senate to put off further debate on ratifying the SALT II agreement. (The agreement was never ratified.) The following month he urged the United States Olympic team to boycott (refuse to attend) the 1980 Olympic Games in Moscow. The president also approved secret aid to Afghan militias who were opposing the Soviet invasion.

Eager to bring an end to the painful hostage crisis, Carter worked with military advisers on a daring rescue plan. The plan was set in motion in April 1980. Transport planes carried supplies and a 90-member rescue crew to a makeshift landing area in the Iranian desert called Desert One. Eight helicopters took off from a carrier in the Gulf of Oman and landed at the site. The plan called for rescuers to enter Tehran in trucks and attack the embassy compound where the hostages were held. Long before the assault, however, the plan unraveled. One helicopter developed mechanical trouble, and a second got lost in a sandstorm. At Desert One another helicopter broke down. With only five helicopters remaining, the commander canceled the mission. As the teams began to depart, disaster struck. A helicopter collided with one of the transport planes, and eight servicemen were killed. The rest of the rescue team returned from the desert in defeat.

The failure of the rescue mission left Carter deeply shaken. He remained in seclusion in the White House, anguished and discouraged. According to the polls, only 21 percent of the public thought he was doing a good job as president. No other president, not even Nixon during the Watergate scandals, had received such a low rating. It was as though the revolutionaries in Tehran had taken Carter and his administration hostage along with the 53 captives.

The timing could not have been worse for Carter. The presidential election in which he hoped to gain another term was just over six months away.

The Last Campaign

Carter entered the election season without control of his own party. In the Democratic primaries, he was opposed by Senator Ted Kennedy, the brother of former president John F. Kennedy. Carter lost the New York primary to Kennedy but soon regained his footing and won the Democratic nomination on the first ballot. Once again Walter Mondale was his running mate. The Republican party chose Ronald Reagan to run for president. Reagan was a popular spokesman for the conservatives who had taken over the Republican party since the end of Gerald Ford's presidency. A moderate Republican named John Anderson also ran as a third-party candidate.

Inflation and unemployment had haunted Carter's term in office. But in the summer of 1980 the economy began to recover, strengthening his appeal to voters. In addition, many Americans had

Republican presidential nominee Ronald Reagan and his wife Nancy wave to crowds at the Republican convention in July 1980.

grave doubts about Ronald Reagan. He had begun his career as a Hollywood actor in the 1930s. Even though he had served eight years as governor of California, some doubted that a former film star was really qualified to lead the nation. As the campaign got under way, pollsters found that Carter and Reagan were almost tied, with Anderson trailing far behind.

In campaign appearances Carter stressed his plans for the next four years. He would work to cut inflation and balance the budget. He would tackle

America's urban problems and build stronger alliances abroad. He also focused on Reagan's weaknesses. He warned that Reagan lacked experience, was closely tied to big business, and had little commitment to social programs.

Meanwhile, however, the American hostages were still held captive in the American embassy in Iran. Only in October did the Ayatollah Khomeini begin to discuss their release. An end to the crisis in Tehran could boost Carter's standing with the voters and undermine the Reagan campaign. Carter believed he had reached an agreement with the Iranian government, but at the last moment, final approval was withheld by Iranian leaders.

To unseat Carter, Reagan had to show his skills as a political leader. He pressed the Carter campaign for televised debates. Carter resisted, sensing that they could only help Reagan, the less familiar candidate. Finally Carter agreed to meet Reagan in Cleveland, Ohio, for a single 90-minute debate on October 28, just a week before the election.

From the opening minutes of the debate, Reagan had the upper hand. He spoke with confidence and sincerity, and his manner radiated a fatherly warmth. Carter seemed to wander off course. At one point he explained that he had asked his daughter Amy what she considered the most important issue facing the United States. Amy had replied, "Nuclear weaponry and the control of nuclear arms." Carter hoped that his mention of Amy would humanize his image, showing him as caring and accessible. His strategy had the opposite effect. Commentators and cartoonists ridiculed him for turning to a teenager on matters of national policy.

At the close of the debate Reagan faced the audience and asked a series of questions. "Are you better off than you were four years ago?" he inquired. "Is it easier for you to go buy things in the stores than it was four years ago? Is there more or less unemployment in the country than there was four years ago? Is America as respected throughout the world as it was? Do you feel that . . . we're as strong as we were four years ago?" Reagan concluded by saying that if the answer to these questions was no, then he "could suggest another choice" for the White House.

The debate had a devastating impact on Carter's chances. In the days before the election Reagan rose steadily in the polls. Hundreds of thousands of undecided voters made Reagan their final choice. On election day Reagan received nearly 51 percent of the popular vote, while Jimmy Carter received only 41 percent. Less than 7 percent went to John Anderson. In the electoral college, Reagan's victory was overwhelming. He collected 489 votes to Carter's 49.

Carter had entered the White House with buoyant spirits, confident that he could make a positive difference in the nation and in the world. Now the people had spoken and told him they wanted someone else to lead them. Carter felt he had failed the people of America, and failed himself as well. Yet, during his last weeks as president, he did his best to promote causes in which he believed.

A solemn Jimmy Carter concedes the presidential election to Ronald Reagan in November 1980.

The Electoral College

As outlined by the U.S. Constitution, the outcome of a presidential election is not determined by adding up the number of popular votes each candidate receives. Voters are actually casting votes for presidential electors from their state. These electors make up the *electoral college*, where the president is actually elected. A state has as many electors as it has U.S. senators and U.S. representatives in Congress. States with large populations like California and Texas have many electors, while states with small populations have only a few. (The District of Columbia also has three electors even though it has no voting representatives in Congress.)

In most states, the presidential candidate who wins the most popular votes wins all of the state's electoral votes. Because of this winner-take-all practice in choosing state electors, a candidate can receive the most popular votes in the nation but fail to be elected president by the electoral college.

☆ ☆ ☆

On November 12, 1980, Congress passed the Alaska Lands bill. Carter strongly supported this legislation, which set aside vast tracts of land in Alaska for protection within the national park system. Carter also helped pass legislation establishing a "Superfund" of $1.6 billion to clean up the nation's most dangerous toxic waste sites.

Carter had also completed negotiations for the release of the American hostages in Iran. Carter was hopeful that the hostages would come home while he was still in office, but the government of Iran refused to release them until a few hours after Ronald Reagan became president on January 20, 1981. The next day, Carter's first day as a private citizen, he flew to Wiesbaden, Germany. There he greeted the returning hostages, who were receiving medical examinations at a U.S. army hospital. Carter had worked ceaselessly to secure their freedom. Now he met them face to face and received their heartfelt thanks. The last mission of his presidency was accomplished.

One day after Ronald Reagan's inauguration, former president Carter meets with hostages released from Iran in a U.S. military hospital in Germany.

A Voice for Peace

Jimmy and Rosalynn Carter returned to Plains and tried to pick up the pieces of their lives. For months they reeled under the shock of Carter's defeat. "It didn't seem fair that everything we had hoped for, all our plans and dreams for the country, could have been gone when the votes were counted," Rosalynn Carter told a reporter.

Carter made few public appearances during his first years back in Plains. He taught classes at Emory University in Atlanta. He also discovered that he had a flair for writing. In a memoir, *Keeping Faith*, he recounted his experiences in the White House.

Soon Carter realized that he did not have to abandon his hopes for the country and the world after all. In 1984 construction got under way on a complex of buildings in Atlanta. Part of the site is occupied by the Jimmy Carter Library and Museum, which is administered by the National Archives and Records Administration. It serves as a repository for Carter's presidential papers. The rest of the site is taken up by the Jimmy Carter Center, a private not-for-profit organization affiliated with Emory University. For more than 20 years, Carter helped direct the work of the center, which has three major aims: "to wage peace, to fight disease, and to bring hope" to the poor of the world.

Since 1985 world-renowned experts and heads of state have attended retreats at the Carter Center to discuss hunger, health care, arms control, the environment, and other critical issues. Teams from the center travel the world, observing and monitoring democratic elections.

Carter's status as a former president and his record of working for peace put him in a unique position. He was welcomed by heads of state all over the world. Though he had no official role in the U.S. government, Carter sometimes acted as a diplomat to help resolve international crises. One of his most successful negotiations occurred in Haiti. In September 1991, General Raoul Cedras ousted Haiti's elected president, Jean-Bertrand Aristide, in a military takeover. Three years later, U.S. president Bill Clinton threatened to use force against Cedras unless he gave up power to President Aristide. U.S. armed forces were poised to intervene. Before the forces landed, Carter visited Haiti and persuaded Cedras to give up power and leave the country without a fight. Carter's efforts prevented a serious military confrontation. President Aristide assumed power once again within weeks.

Another concern of the Carter Center was the control of infectious disease. Carter was especially interested in diseases that were widespread in Africa. In several African countries the Carter Center made strides toward eliminating

Above, the former president monitors elections in Indonesia for the Carter Center. At right, Jimmy and Rosalynn at work building affordable houses with Habitat for Humanity in Miami, Florida.

river blindness, an eye disease carried by tiny flies. The center also worked to reduce Guinea worm disease, a condition caused by parasites.

Closer to home, Carter became active in Habitat for Humanity, an organization that builds sturdy, inexpensive housing for homeless families. Carter sawed lumber, hammered nails, and painted ceilings. After his first day on a Habitat work crew in Americus, Georgia, the *New York Times* reported, "Mr. Carter has been toiling in a callous-raising enterprise that may be unheard-of for a former commander-in-chief."

Carter became a prolific writer during his post-White House years. He published several memoirs as well as books on foreign affairs, religion, and his personal philosophy. He has published two volumes of poetry. In 2003 he became the first U.S. president ever to publish a work of fiction. His novel, *The Hornet's Nest*, tells the story of a fictional Georgia family at the time of the American Revolution.

The Finest Former President

Most historians agree that Carter's presidency was largely unsuccessful. During his years in the White House he was often indecisive, tossed about on a sea of conflicting opinions. His strong emphasis on human rights in other countries was

Carter chats with Cuban president Fidel Castro on a baseball field during his historic visit to Cuba in May 2002.

largely ineffective and sometimes complicated U.S. diplomacy. During his term, the U.S. economy suffered from high inflation and growing unemployment. Despite his intentions to balance the budget, the United States sank deeper into

Carter receives the Nobel Peace Prize for his many contributions to world peace in December 2002.

debt during his administration. Faced with major foreign challenges in Iran and Afghanistan, he seemed powerless to achieve U.S. goals there. Perhaps most seriously, the American people gradually lost confidence in his leadership.

Carter will be remembered for his central role in achieving the Camp David Accords, which seemed to begin a new era in Middle Eastern affairs. At home, he extended regulations to protect the environment and appointed more women and ethnic minorities to high government positions than any previous president.

In the end, however, Jimmy Carter may be remembered more for his accomplishments *after* he left the presidency than for his achievements in office. One commentator called him "the best former president the nation has ever had." In 1998 he received one of the first United Nations Human Rights Prizes. That same year, he and Rosalynn jointly won the Presidential Medal of Freedom, the highest civilian award granted by the U.S. government.

On October 11, 2002, the Nobel Prize committee announced that Carter would be awarded the 2002 Nobel Peace Prize. He accepted the prize at a ceremony in Oslo, Norway, later that year. He received the award for "his decades of untiring efforts to find peaceful solutions to international conflicts." He could receive no greater honor, no more enduring recognition of his achievements.

James Earl Carter Jr.

Birth:	October 1, 1924
Birthplace:	Plains, Georgia
Parents:	James Earl Carter and Lillian Gordy Carter
Brother & Sisters:	Gloria (1926–1990)
	Ruth (1929–1983)
	William Alton "Billy" (1937–1988)
Education:	U.S. Naval Academy, graduated 1946
Occupation:	U.S. naval officer; farmer-businessman
Marriage:	To Eleanor Rosalynn Smith, July 7, 1946
Children:	(*see* First Lady Fast Facts at right)
Political Party:	Democratic
Government Service:	1963–1967 Georgia State Senator
	1971–1975 Governor of Georgia
	1977–1981 39th President of the United States
His Vice President:	Walter F. Mondale
Major Actions as President:	1977 Declared an amnesty for Vietnam War draft evaders
	1977 Established new Department of Energy
	1978 Announced Camp David Accords between Israel and Egypt
	1979 Began negotiations with Iran for release of U.S. hostages
	1980 Protested Soviet invasion of Afghanistan by U.S. boycott of Summer Olympics in Moscow
	1980 Ordered unsuccessful attempt to rescue hostages in Iran
	1981 Completed negotiation to free U.S. hostages
Firsts:	First native of Georgia elected president
	First former U.S. Navy officer elected president
	First president to walk from the Capitol to the White House after his inauguration

Fast Facts

Eleanor Rosalynn Smith Carter

Birth:	August 18, 1927
Birthplace:	Plains, Georgia
Parents:	Wilburn Edgar Smith and Frances Allethea Murray Smith
Brothers & Sisters:	Two younger brothers, Jerry and Murray
	One younger sister, Lillian Allethea
Education:	Attended Georgia Southwestern College, 1942–1944
Marriage:	To James Earl Carter Jr., July 7, 1946
Children:	John William "Jack" (1947–)
	James Earl "Chip" (1950–)
	Donnel Jeffrey "Jeff" (1952–)
	Amy Lynn Carter (1967–)
Firsts:	First to win Presidential Medal of Freedom (together with her husband), 1998

Timeline

1924	1928	1941	1941	1942
James Earl Carter Jr. born in Plains, Georgia, October 1.	Family moves to farm near Archery, Georgia. 	Carter graduates from Plains High School; enters Georgia Southwestern College, September.	U.S. enters World War II after Japanese attack on Pearl Harbor, December.	Carter studies at Georgia Institute of Technology.

1951	1952	1953	1962	1966
Carter serves on new submarine *K-1*.	Trains to serve on a nuclear-powered submarine; son Jeff born.	Gives up navy commission after father's death, returns to family farm business in Georgia. 	Elected to the Georgia state senate, serves 1963–1967. 	Defeated for governor in Democratic primary election.

1978	1979	1980	1981	1985
Helps negotiate Camp David Accords, agreements between Israel and Egypt. 	Revolutionaries in Iran take U.S. embassy staff hostage. 	Attempt to rescue hostages in Iran fails, April; Carter nominated for re-election, August; loses election to Republican Ronald Reagan, November.	Carter returns to Plains, Georgia.	Carter Center opens in Atlanta.

1943	1946	1947	1948	1950
Enters U.S. Naval Academy at Annapolis, Maryland.	Graduates from Naval Academy; marries Rosalynn Smith.	Son Jack born.	Carter trains to become a submarine officer.	Son Chip born.

1967	1970	1974	1976	1977
Daughter Amy born.	Carter elected governor of Georgia, serves 1971–1975.	President Nixon resigns from office; Gerald Ford becomes president.	Carter nominated by Democrats for president, July; defeats Gerald Ford, November.	Inaugurated as 39th president; issues amnesty to Vietnam War draft evaders; establishes new Department of Energy.

1994	2002
Carter helps negotiate peaceful resolution to conflict in Haiti.	Awarded the Nobel Peace Prize.

Glossary

amnesty: pardon; freedom from prosecution for real or suspected wrongdoing in the past

boycott: a group action refusing to deal with a business or government to protest an injustice

decommission: take out of military service

dissident: a person who speaks out against the actions or policies of a government

impeachment: a process in which Congress brings formal charges against a public official; if convicted of the charges, the official is removed from office

integration: ending segregation; bringing all groups into full membership in society

legislature: the lawmaking body of a state or country; Congress is the national legislature in the United States

mandatory: required by rule or by law

mediator: a go-between; a neutral person who helps disagreeing parties reach an agreement or settlement

primary election: an election through which a political party determines its candidate for an office; the candidate then runs against candidates of other parties in the general election

revival: a series of church services encouraging Christians to renew their faith through a personal experience of God's power and love

segregation: separation of people based on a special characteristic such as race or religion

Further Reading

Schraff, Anne E. *Jimmy Carter*. Springfield, NJ: Enslow Publishers, 1998.

Seidman, David. *Jimmy Carter*. New York: Franklin Watts, 2004.

Slavicek, Louise Chipley. *Jimmy Carter*. Philadelphia: Chelsea House, 2004.

Stein, R. Conrad. *The Iran Hostage Crisis*. Chicago: Children's Press, 1994.

Weiss, Ellen, and Mel Friedman. *Jimmy Carter: Champion of Peace*. New York: Aladdin Paperbacks, 2003.

MORE ADVANCED READING

Bourne, Peter G. *Jimmy Carter: A Comprehensive Biography, from Plains to Post-Presidency*. New York: Scribner, 1997.

Brinkley, Douglas. *The Unfinished Presidency: Jimmy Carter's Journey beyond the White House*. New York: Viking, 1998.

Carter, Jimmy. *An Hour Before Daylight: Memoirs of a Rural Boyhood*. New York: Simon & Schuster, 2001.

——. *Conversations with Carter*. Edited by Don Richardson. New York: Lynn Rhiner Publishers, 1998.

——. *Keeping Faith: Memoirs of a President*. New York: Bantam Books, 1982.

——. *Why Not the Best?* Nashville: Broadman Press, 1977.

Kaufman, Burton I. *The Presidency of James Earl Carter Jr*. Lawrence: The University Press of Kansas, 1993.

Wooten, James T. *Dasher: The Roots and the Rising of Jimmy Carter*. New York: Summit Books, 1978.

Places to Visit

★ ★ ★ ★ ★

Jimmy Carter Library and Museum

441 Freedom Parkway

Atlanta, GA 30307

(404) 865-7100

In addition to archives of Carter's life and presidency, the library and museum host rotating exhibits on presidential history and lore. Carter's Nobel Peace Prize is on display.

Jimmy Carter National Historic Site

300 N. Bond Street

Plains, GA 31780

Visitor Information: (229) 824-4104

Operated by the National Park Service, this site includes the Plains Depot, which served as Carter's campaign headquarters in 1976; the Jimmy Carter Boyhood Farm Museum; and the Plains High School Museum.

Online Sites of Interest

★ **The White House**

www.whitehouse.gov/history/presidents/jc39.html

Biographical information about Carter and the history of his presidency.

★ **The Carter Center**

www.cartercenter.org

Information about the history and goals of the Carter Center.

★ **The Jimmy Carter Library and Museum**

www.jimmycarterlibrary.org

Information about the library and museum, and archival material about Carter's life and administration.

★ **The American Experience**

www.pbs.org/wgbh/amex/carter/

Materials accompanying a televised documentary on Jimmy Carter on the PBS series *The American Experience*. Contains an excellent timeline of his life.

★ **The Jimmy Carter National Historical Site**

www.nps.gov/jica/

Information about the site, which includes the farm he grew up on and landmarks in Plains, Georgia.

★ **The Nobel Peace Prize**

www.nobel.se/peace/laureates/2002/

Provides the citation naming Carter as a winner in 2002 and the full text of his acceptance speech.

★ **Habitat for Humanity**

www.habitat.org/how/carter.html

Information on the role Jimmy Carter has played in supporting and expanding this organization.

Table of Presidents

	1. George Washington	2. John Adams	3. Thomas Jefferson	4. James Madison
Took office	Apr 30 1789	Mar 4 1797	Mar 4 1801	Mar 4 1809
Left office	Mar 3 1797	Mar 3 1801	Mar 3 1809	Mar 3 1817
Birthplace	Westmoreland Co, VA	Braintree, MA	Shadwell, VA	Port Conway, VA
Birth date	Feb 22 1732	Oct 20 1735	Apr 13 1743	Mar 16 1751
Death date	Dec 14 1799	July 4 1826	July 4 1826	June 28 1836

	9. William H. Harrison	10. John Tyler	11. James K. Polk	12. Zachary Taylor
Took office	Mar 4 1841	Apr 6 1841	Mar 4 1845	Mar 5 1849
Left office	**Apr 4 1841•**	Mar 3 1845	Mar 3 1849	**July 9 1850•**
Birthplace	Berkeley, VA	Greenway, VA	Mecklenburg Co, NC	Barboursville, VA
Birth date	Feb 9 1773	Mar 29 1790	Nov 2 1795	Nov 24 1784
Death date	Apr 4 1841	Jan 18 1862	June 15 1849	July 9 1850

	17. Andrew Johnson	18. Ulysses S. Grant	19. Rutherford B. Hayes	20. James A. Garfield
Took office	Apr 15 1865	Mar 4 1869	Mar 5 1877	Mar 4 1881
Left office	Mar 3 1869	Mar 3 1877	Mar 3 1881	**Sept 19 1881•**
Birthplace	Raleigh, NC	Point Pleasant, OH	Delaware, OH	Orange, OH
Birth date	Dec 29 1808	Apr 27 1822	Oct 4 1822	Nov 19 1831
Death date	July 31 1875	July 23 1885	Jan 17 1893	Sept 19 1881

5. James Monroe	6. John Quincy Adams	7. Andrew Jackson	8. Martin Van Buren
Mar 4 1817	Mar 4 1825	Mar 4 1829	Mar 4 1837
Mar 3 1825	Mar 3 1829	Mar 3 1837	Mar 3 1841
Westmoreland Co, VA	Braintree, MA	The Waxhaws, SC	Kinderhook, NY
Apr 28 1758	July 11 1767	Mar 15 1767	Dec 5 1782
July 4 1831	Feb 23 1848	June 8 1845	July 24 1862

13. Millard Fillmore	14. Franklin Pierce	15. James Buchanan	16. Abraham Lincoln
July 9 1850	Mar 4 1853	Mar 4 1857	Mar 4 1861
Mar 3 1853	Mar 3 1857	Mar 3 1861	**Apr 15 1865•**
Locke Township, NY	Hillsborough, NH	Cove Gap, PA	Hardin Co, KY
Jan 7 1800	Nov 23 1804	Apr 23 1791	Feb 12 1809
Mar 8 1874	Oct 8 1869	June 1 1868	Apr 15 1865

21. Chester A. Arthur	22. Grover Cleveland	23. Benjamin Harrison	24. Grover Cleveland
Sept 19 1881	Mar 4 1885	Mar 4 1889	Mar 4 1893
Mar 3 1885	Mar 3 1889	Mar 3 1893	Mar 3 1897
Fairfield, VT	Caldwell, NJ	North Bend, OH	Caldwell, NJ
Oct 5 1829	Mar 18 1837	Aug 20 1833	Mar 18 1837
Nov 18 1886	June 24 1908	Mar 13 1901	June 24 1908

	25. William McKinley	26. Theodore Roosevelt	27. William H. Taft	28. Woodrow Wilson
Took office	Mar 4 1897	Sept 14 1901	Mar 4 1909	Mar 4 1913
Left office	Sept 14 1901•	Mar 3 1909	Mar 3 1913	Mar 3 1921
Birthplace	Niles, OH	New York, NY	Cincinnati, OH	Staunton, VA
Birth date	Jan 29 1843	Oct 27 1858	Sept 15 1857	Dec 28 1856
Death date	Sept 14 1901	Jan 6 1919	Mar 8 1930	Feb 3 1924

	33. Harry S. Truman	34. Dwight D. Eisenhower	35. John F. Kennedy	36. Lyndon B. Johnson
Took office	Apr 12 1945	Jan 20 1953	Jan 20 1961	Nov 22 1963
Left office	Jan 20 1953	Jan 20 1961	Nov 22 1963•	Jan 20 1969
Birthplace	Lamar, MO	Denison, TX	Brookline, MA	Johnson City, TX
Birth date	May 8 1884	Oct 14 1890	May 29 1917	Aug 27 1908
Death date	Dec 26 1972	Mar 28 1969	Nov 22 1963	Jan 22 1973

	41. George Bush	42. Bill Clinton	43. George W. Bush
Took office	Jan 20 1989	Jan 20 1993	Jan 20 2001
Left office	Jan 20 1993	Jan 20 2001	—
Birthplace	Milton, MA	Hope, AR	New Haven, CT
Birth date	June 12 1924	Aug 19 1946	July 6 1946
Death date	—	—	—

29. Warren G. Harding	30. Calvin Coolidge	31. Herbert Hoover	32. Franklin D. Roosevelt
Mar 4 1921	Aug 2 1923	Mar 4 1929	Mar 4 1933
Aug 2 1923•	Mar 3 1929	Mar 3 1933	**Apr 12 1945•**
Blooming Grove, OH	Plymouth, VT	West Branch, IA	Hyde Park, NY
Nov 21 1865	July 4 1872	Aug 10 1874	Jan 30 1882
Aug 2 1923	Jan 5 1933	Oct 20 1964	Apr 12 1945

37. Richard M. Nixon	38. Gerald R. Ford	39. Jimmy Carter	40. Ronald Reagan
Jan 20 1969	Aug 9 1974	Jan 20 1977	Jan 20 1981
Aug 9 1974★	Jan 20 1977	Jan 20 1981	Jan 20 1989
Yorba Linda, CA	Omaha, NE	Plains, GA	Tampico, IL
Jan 9 1913	July 14 1913	Oct 1 1924	Feb 6 1911
Apr 22 1994	—	—	June 5 2004

• Indicates the president died while in office.

★ Richard Nixon resigned before his term expired.

Index

Page numbers in *italics* indicate illustrations.

Afghanistan, 78, 95
African Americans, 13–14, 40–41, 51
Agnew, Spiro, 52
Alaska Lands bill, 86
Americus, Georgia, 19, 24, 28, 92
amnesty, 65
Anderson, John, 81, 84
Archery, Georgia, 7, *8*
Atomic Energy Commission, U.S., 36
Ayatollah Khomeini, 75, 83

Baptists, 14, 16
Begin, Menachem, 72–73, *73*
boycott, 40, 78
Brezhnev, Leonid, 75
Brown v. Board of Education, 40
Byrd, Robert, 68

Camp David Accords, 72–73, 95
Carter, Amy, 33, 45, *60*, 83
Carter, Billy, 9, 44
Carter, Earl, 7, 10, 16, 23, 36
Carter, Jimmy (James Earl, Jr.), *20*, *30*, *35*, *66*, *85*
    and Camp David Accords, 72–73, *73*, 95
    campaign for governor, 44–46
    campaign for president 1976, 51–52, 54–61, *55*, *57*
    campaign for president 1980, 81–84
    campaign for state senator, 42–43
    early life, 7–13, *11*, *15*
    education, 19–21, 24, 26
    family, 9, 31, 33, 36, 45
    fast facts, 96
    as governor, 47–52, *48*, *50*

and Habitat for Humanity, *91*, 92
honors and awards, 95
and hostage crisis in Iran, 76–78, 79, 83, 86–87, *87*
and international relations, 71–79
and Iran, 74–79, 83, 86–87, 95
life after presidency, 88–95, *90*, *93*
marriage, 29
in navy, 31–36, *29*, 38
and Nobel Peace Prize, *94*, 95
political campaign, 42–44
as president, *60*, 63–79, *64*, *68*
religion, 14, 16, 38, 45
returns to farming, 37–41, *39*
in state senate, 44
as submariner, 33–36
timeline, 98–99
at U.S. Naval Academy, 26–28
as writer, 88, 92
Carter, Lillian, 7, 9–10, *11*, 23, *29*, *66*
Carter, Rosalynn
    children, 31, 33
    contribution to family business, 38
    fast facts, 97
    as first lady. *60*, 61, 63, *64*, *74*, *85*
    life after the White House, 88, *91*
    marriage, 29, *30*
    Presidential Medal of Freedom, 95
    See also Rosalynn Smith
civil rights, 40
consumer affairs, 67
Cuba, *93*

dam projects, 67
debates, 61, 83
Democratic party, 16, 18, 42, 45, 46, 51, 54, 67, 81

desegregation, 49
draft dodgers, 65

Egypt, 72–73
election reform, 44
electoral college, 61, 86
electricity, 16
Energy, Department of, 69
environment, 95

Ford, Gerald
    campaign for president 1976, 56, 58–61
    early career, 59
    as president, 53–54, *53*
    as vice president, 52
    view on draft resisters, 65
Future Farmers of America, 15, 21

gasoline, 75–76
Goldwater, Barry, 65
Gordy, Tom, 23

Habitat for Humanity, *91*, 92
Haiti, 89
health care, 67
hostage crisis in Iran, 76–78, 79, 83, 86–87,
    87
human rights, 71, 92

inflation, 81, 82, 93
integration, 41, 45, 49
Iran, 74–79, 83, 86–87, 95
Israel, 71–72

Jimmy Carter Center, 88–92
Jimmy Carter Library and Museum, 88
Jordan, Hamilton, 52, 65

King, Martin Luther, Jr., 40, 51

Lance, Bert, 65, 70, *71*

Maddox, Lester, 45, *48*, 49
McGovern, George, 51
mental health services, 49
Middle East, 71–73, 95
Miss Lillian. *See* Carter, Lillian
Mondale, Walter, 56, 81

Naval Academy, U.S., 24, 26–28
New Deal, 17, 18
Nixon, Richard, 51, 52–54, 59, 79
Nobel Peace Prize, 73, *94*, 95

oil, 69, 76
O'Neill, Thomas "Tip," 67–68, *68*
Olympic Games, 78

Pace, Stephen, 24, 26
Palestine, 72
Peace Corps, 66
peace work, 89, 94
peanuts, 7, *39*, *55*
Plains, Georgia, 7, 9, 14, 16, 23, 36, 37, 41,
    88
Powell, Jody, 65

Reagan, Ronald, 56, 81–85, *82*, 87
Republican party, 52, 56, 81
Rickover, Hyman, 34, *35*, 54
Roosevelt, Franklin D., 16, 18

Sadat, Anwar al-, 72–73, *73*
SALT II (Strategic Arms Limitation Treaty),
    75, 78
Schlesinger, James, 69
segregation, 13–14, 40–41, 47
Shah of Iran, *74*, 74–79
sharecroppers, 12, 13

Smith, Rosalynn, 28–30. *See also* Carter, Rosalynn
Social Security, 67
Soviet Union, 61, 71, 75, 78
Superfund, 86

Talmadge, Eugene, 17, *18*
tax reform, 67

unemployment, 81, 93

Vietnam War, 65
voter fraud, 43

Watergate affair, 52–53, 56, 79
welfare reform, 67, 69
White Citizens Councils, 41, 45

About the Author

Deborah Kent grew up in Little Falls, New Jersey. She received her B.A. in English from Oberlin College, in northeastern Ohio. She earned a master's degree from Smith College School for Social Work.

After four years as a social worker at the University Settlement House in New York City, Ms. Kent moved to San Miguel de Allende in Mexico to try her hand at writing. While living in Mexico she completed her first novel, *Belonging*. Ms. Kent is the author of 18 young-adult novels and numerous nonfiction titles for middle-grade readers. She lives in Chicago with her husband, children's book author R. Conrad Stein, and their daughter Janna.